P9-DEP-810

Hey There,

Leslie Bulion

ini Charlesbridge

Stink Bug!

Illustrated by Leslie Evans

For Rubin—L. B.

To Charlie—L. E.

Text copyright © 2006 by Leslie Bulion
Illustrations copyright © 2006 by Leslie Evans
All rights reserved, including the right of reproduction in whole or in part in any
form. Charlesbridge and colophon are registered trademarks of Charlesbridge
Publishing, Inc.

Published by Charlesbridge
85 Main Street
Watertown, MA 02472
(617) 926-0329
www.charlesbridge.com

Library of Congress Cataloging-in-Publication Data
Bulion, Leslie, 1958–
    Hey there, stink bug! / by Leslie Bulion; illustrated by Leslie Evans.
       p. cm.
    Summary: "Describes various types of insects using different poetic forms.
Includes glossary and poetry notes"—Provided by publisher.
    ISBN-13: 978-1-58089-304-6; ISBN-10: 1-58089-304-X (reinforced for library use)
    1. Insects—Juvenile literature. I. Evans, Leslie, 1953– ill. II. Title.
QL467.2.B85 2006
595.7—dc22   2005019627

Printed in China
(hc) 10 9 8 7 6 5 4 3 2 1

Illustrations made from linoleum block prints and watercolor on Arches paper
Display type set in Quetzalcoatl; text type set in Weiss and Humana Sans
Color separations by Chroma Graphics
Printed and bound by Everbest Printing Company, Ltd.,
    through Four Colour Imports, Ltd., Louisville, Kentucky
Production supervision by Brian G. Walker
Designed by Susan Mallory Sherman

Contents

Go Buggy!

Do you
think butterflies are ornamental?
Are marching ants just accidental?
Are lady beetles sentimental?
Take a closer look.

They've spent
four hundred million years evolving
elegant, devious tricks, involving
bug-get-buggy problem solving.
Take a closer look.

They can
bug-hunt each other on chemical cue,
play dead, spin thread, turn guts to stew,
boast two hundred million per one of you.
Take a closer look.

This is
an insect world with humans in it.
We'll seize the day, but they will win it.
You've been forewarned, now let's begin it—
Take a closer look . . .

at BUGS!

Hey There, Stink Bug!

PUPUPUPUPUPUPU   PUPUPUPUPUPU   PUPUPUPUPUPU   PUPUPUPUP UPUPUPU

Hey
there, stink
bug! What do you think,
bug? I'm not a bird or a lizard or a bat.
You're not a treat that I'm wanting
to eat. I'm just watching you lunch
on your leaf habitat. Uh-oh, stink
bug! Know what I think, bug? I
think you're lost 'cause you're
walking up my arm. But I won't
tease you, wouldn't dare
squeeze you—please don't
trigger your stink
alarm!

When stink bugs are scared, they let loose a stinky fluid that oozes from two holes on their underside.

A tiny whiff of the chemicals in stink bug fluid might smell almost sweet. But the stink bug's mixture is so strong that it smells awful.

Stink bugs lay their eggs in bunches. Their eggs stink, too, and predators get the warning: Stay away!

Multiplication

An aphid has a sharpened snout
to stab then slurp a plant's sap out,
but that is not her habit most unfriendly.

To help her drain that poor plant dry
she clones more little aphid fry,
who squirt out by the dozens, other-endly.

When an insect makes an exact copy of itself,
that's a kind of cloning called parthenogenesis.

Aphids are born with live daughters already
developing inside of them. Those daughters
have daughters inside, too. One of these little
plant suckers can create an enormous, thirsty
family very quickly!

It is lucky for plants that aphids are the favorite
snack of such helpful insects as ladybugs.

The Hot Shot

Bombardier bombardier bombardier beetle,
slow on the wing but thinks fast on its feetle.
Blasting poor predators into retreatle,
with boiling hot acid it aims from its seatle.

When an enemy bothers a bombardier beetle,
two chemicals mix inside the beetle and explode
with a pop into acid spray.

The bombardier beetle has great aim and can
fire its spray in any direction.

Birds, mice, lizards, and even ants work hard to
rub off the bombardier beetle's burning acid.

Flies

Mayfly
dragonfly
firefly
and
butterfly.

One-word fly name, four fine wings;
true flies never have these things.

House fly
bottle fly
flesh fly
and
soldier fly.

Two-word name, one pair of wings;
real flies breed on ghastly things.

Cow manure
hog manure
roadkill corpse
an open sewer.

Other nests would be much neater;
but a hatching maggot's a picky eater.

A maggot is the young, wormlike form of a fly and some other two-winged insects. It's what hatches from the fly's egg.

Adult flies lay eggs in stinky spots where hatchlings can easily burrow right into their soft and often rotting food.

Like its flashier cousin the caterpillar, who metamorphoses into a butterfly, a maggot will transform into a pupa, and then become an adult fly.

Japanese Beetle

Gone are rosebud dreams.
A bronze-green jewel flies
into my ear.

Japanese beetles are good fliers. Like all beetles, their flying wings are tucked under hard wing covers called elytra. The bodies and elytra of Japanese beetles are very shiny.

Japanese beetles choose the hundreds of types of plants they eat by smell.

Japanese beetles munch the soft parts of leaves, flowers, and fruit. Chemicals released from the chewed parts send a message to other Japanese beetles: Come eat!

Making Scents

It isn't
that the skipper caterpillar
wants
his leaf house
that he skillfully strings together
with sticky silk,
to stay spotless
and tidy.

It isn't
that the skipper caterpillar
wants
every bit of the space
in his leafy homemade hideaway
all for his apple-green-striped wriggly
self.

The reason
that the skipper caterpillar
is
a
jet propeller
frass
expeller
IS
that
those frass pellets he force-fires far from his caterpillar fanny
smell
as good as hot-from-the-oven chocolate-chip cookies
to enemy paper wasps
and others

who would come and gobble up
that wily skipper
if he didn't make sure
that their smellers
would lead them

        someplace

           else.

Frass is the name scientists use for solid food waste that comes out of the back end of an insect. Some predators, like paper wasps, use the smell of frass to find their food.

Skipper butterfly caterpillars shoot their frass pellets more than three feet away from their homes. Hungry wasps are fooled into looking in the wrong place for a bite to eat.

Skippers wrap silk around leaves to make a tiny tent. Predators who want a caterpillar meal might not find the caterpillar under the leaves.

Nightmare

I dreamed a spider from the ceiling
dropped into my mouth.
I didn't see him loose his line
and start to bungee south.

I dreamed he crawled across my tongue,
I dreamed his silk thread followed.
But it was worse for him than me
when I woke up and swallowed.

Spider silk is strong and flexible. All spiders spin silk, but not all spiders weave webs.

Spiders use silk to make cases for their eggs, to line holes in the ground, to wrap their prey, and to attach a dragline to something in case they have to jump away from danger.

Some spiderweb silk is sticky to trap small insects. The long strands of silk that hold a web in place are not sticky. Spiders walk across their webs on the nonsticky strands of silk.

Antlion

Doodlebug
       doodles
         a
             trail in
                   the sand
                       while it
          finds a nice spot
           for its funnel-
            shaped
             pit.

In
    falls
       an
          ant   who is

grabbed-stabbed-and-poisoned,
its juices sucked out and then out ant is   spit.

               PTOO!

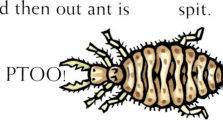

Doodlebug is a nickname for the young form of a flying insect called an antlion. Can you guess how it got its nickname?

Many insects look quite different when they first hatch. The young form of an insect, called a larva, can change size or shape several times before it becomes an adult.

An antlion larva is a ferocious predator of ants and other crawling insects. It hides in the bottom of its pit trap with just the very tips of its sharp, curved jaws showing.

An adult antlion looks a bit like a dragonfly with a smaller head. Its four wings are crisscrossed with veins that look like very fine netting.

Fooled by the Lights

Don't try to warn that firefly dude.
    He's all FLASH FLASH when he flies.
A beetle with lightning-bug attitude
    who could meet a nasty surprise.

He'll fly and he'll FLASH and he'll wait for an answer—
    a FLASH gal who's happy to meet him.
But a sly FLASH impostor could fool that romancer
    and up close she's likely to eat him!

FLASH FLASH chomp chomp BURRRP

Each type of firefly flashes in its own special on-off pattern.

Different types of fireflies flash different colors, from green to yellow to orange.

Many kinds of male fireflies flash their patterns while they fly. The female firefly sits near the ground and watches for a male who is flashing her signal. She'll wait a certain number of seconds, then flash back to call him over.

The female firefly of one tricky species will flash back at a male firefly who's not her type. When he lands nearby, she'll eat him.

Advice to a Caterpillar

Said the swallowtail, "Kid, here's the scoop:
That ravenous robin's a snoop.
Once you pupate you'll be
quite as dazzling as me,
but for now just pretend you're bird poop."

The brightly colored wings of the swallowtail
butterfly remind hungry predators that some
swallowtails taste bad.

The swallowtail's two "tails" at the bottom of
their wings can look like antennae.
If a hungry bird is fooled into biting the wrong
end, the butterfly goes free.

Some swallowtail caterpillars have light and dark
markings that make them look just like bird
droppings. No bird is that hungry!

Swarm

The squashed
yellow jacket
sends this perfume alarm:
Sisters from my underground nest—
come sting!

Yellow jackets are wasps that live in large
colonies. Many build nests near the ground or
underground out of papery bits of old wood
mixed with their own spit.

A painful yellow jacket sting convinces enemies
to go away. The irritating chemicals also send a
message through the air to other yellow jackets
to come and help defend their nest. When a
yellow jacket is squashed, a bigger blast of
chemicals gets into the air.

Wolf Spider Mama

She lurks in darkly secret cracks and crags,
between the rocks or burrowed in the dirt.
Eight eyes, two fangs, most hideous of hags.
A fearsome predator on high alert.

She never trifles with two-legged beasts,
unless a hatchling bird falls near her stoop.
On insects, spiders, frogs, pink mice she feasts,
with poisoned stab she turns their guts to soup.

The eggs inside her sac will hatch one day.
The newborns piggyback in Mother's hair.
When hunters, spiderlings balloon away
on strands of silk to seek their own grim lair.

But if one stays too long on Mother's back,
she'll pierce then pulverize him for a snack.

Wolf spiders have three rows of eyes: four small eyes in a row see things that are close; two very large eyes face forward and can see longer distances; and two large eyes are set a bit back and to the sides to help the spider see upward and backward.

Wolf spiders do not spin webs. They hide on or near the ground, then jump out and chase down their prey.

A female wolf spider wraps and rolls her eggs into a sac of spun silk. She attaches the sac to her back end and drags it behind her.

Dung Beetle

Hard-working scarab
sculpts a tasty ball for grub.
Beetle rock and roll
saves the world from dancing
knee-deep in elephant doo.

Dung beetles belong to a family of wide-bodied
beetles called scarab beetles. Scarabs are often
very colorful.

Dung beetles eat chunks of animal manure,
called dung. Some dung beetles pat the dung
into balls. They kick-roll the balls away and may
even take them underground. Dung beetles are
quite a clean-up crew!

Some dung beetles lay an egg inside their dung
ball. When the caterpillar-like beetle grub
hatches from the egg, the dung ball is both food
and home.

Recycling

Earth needs the bloaty termite queen—
that old wood-in, eggs-out machine.
But still, we humans tend to grouse
When workers feed her pre-chewed house.

Termites live in groups called colonies. Large
termite colonies have lasted a hundred years
and can house up to ten thousand termites.

Some termites build their colonies into giant
mounds of packed dirt. Others chew networks
of tunnels into the wood between the walls of
people's houses.

The termite queen's job is to lay egg after egg.
Soldier termites defend the colony from
invaders. Worker termites feed the king and
queen, the soldiers, and all of the termite larvae.

Thanklessness

Some tiny wasps are sneaky killers
of certain kinds of caterpillars,
injecting wasp eggs stingerly,
which adds insult to injury.

Then mama wasp goes off to play.
Her eggs are safely tucked away
in caterpillar's custody,
which adds insult to injury.

Sir caterpillar eats green leaves,
while each new hatchling bobs and weaves
around in his anatomy,
which adds insult to injury.

As caterpillar crawls about,
wasp larvae munch him inside out.
Such thanks for hospitality,
which adds insult to injury.

When nearly grown, out wasplings burst,
and caterpillar's doubly cursed.
Robbed in and out of dignity,
which adds insult to injury.

Parasitic wasps use their stingers to put their
eggs into the bodies of other insects like bees,
caterpillars, and beetle grubs.

A newly hatched wasp steals all its food from the
body of its host insect. When the wasp larva is
ready to live on its own and change into an adult
wasp, the host dies.

Parasitic wasps don't harm people. Farmers and
gardeners sometimes use them to kill insects
that eat their plants.

Housekeeping

A tortoise beetle larva sits on leaves he loves to eat.
Out spin his stringy droppings, still he keeps his table neat.

He weaves strange ropes of poop and glue, continuing to sup,
a fork behind his hind end and his droppings dropping up.

And though he may seem muddled, topsy-turvy, front to back,
and predators should spot this fool and snarf a tasty snack—

In truth this beetle youngster is a most resourceful fella,
who hides from many enemies beneath his dung umbrella.

Insects that eat tortoise beetle larvae don't seem to notice the larvae when the larvae are under a shelter woven from strings of their droppings.

A forklike prong at the back end of the larva aims the string of droppings above the beetle to the right or to the left to make a thick, woven cover.

There is at least one kind of ground beetle that knows to dig under the stringy cover or chew through it to gobble up the tortoise beetle larva.

Beetlemania

Bigabee, bugabee,
land-dwelling arthropod
species—a million and
still on the rise.

Face it, our planet is
entomological—
may I suggest a nice
beetle disguise?

Entomology is the scientific study of insects.

The animal phylum known as Arthropoda
includes many land dwellers such as insects,
spiders, and centipedes. Other arthropods,
like lobsters, shrimp, and horseshoe crabs,
live in the sea.

Scientists have already identified almost a
million species of insects, and they estimate
there are close to thirty million insect species
on Earth. That's more than all animal species
added together. More beetle species have been
identified than any other kind of insect.

Watch Your Step

It's a bug's world of intrigue and mystery,
with humans a blip in their history.
So when insects flitter and scurry past us
Take note, because they may outlast us!

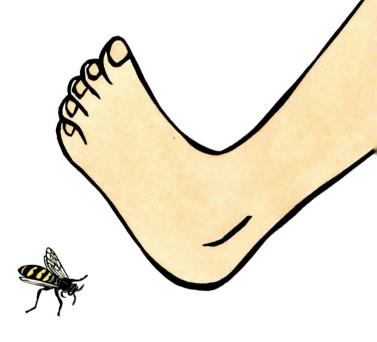

Glossary

anatomy—the structure of an animal's body, including all of the parts; also the study of the structure of an animal's body

antenna—one of two slender, movable sensory organs on top of an insect's head that the insect uses to smell, taste, and, for some insects, hear (two or more antenna are called antennae)

bug—a member of one particular order of insects called Hemiptera that have wings with a thickened, leathery part near the insect's body, and mouths made for sucking, not chewing; often used to include every kind of insect and insectlike animal

chemical cue—a message sent by an insect through making and releasing chemicals from its body that other insects and animals smell, see, or taste

colony—a large group of animals that live together

dragline—a strand of silk a spider uses to attach itself to something, allowing the spider to jump away from danger in a hurry, fall only the length of the line, and then pull itself back up by taking in the line as it goes

dung—animal manure, or solid waste

elytra—the hard outer covers over a beetle's flying wings (a single wing covering is an elytron)

entomology—the scientific study of insects

frass—insect droppings

grub—the wormy, caterpillary young form of a beetle; slang for food

habitat—the place in which an animal finds just the right kind of food, shelter, and climate conditions to live successfully

host—an unrelated plant or animal that a parasite uses for food and/or protection

insect—a small animal that has a hard covering on the outside; a body divided into three parts, or segments; three pairs of legs; and usually two antennae

larva—the young form of an insect that can look quite different from its adult form; for example, a caterpillar looks very different from the butterfly it becomes (two or more larva are called larvae)

maggot—the wormlike larva of a fly that has no legs, and has a head that is not clearly separated from the rest of its body

metamorphosis—the change in an insect from its young form to its adult form during which the insect sometimes changes to a completely different form, like the grub that becomes a beetle; sometimes it grows bigger and develops wings, like the grasshopper

parasite—a plant or animal that depends on an unrelated plant or animal for its food and/or protection and usually harms that plant or animal in the process

parthenogenesis—the kind of cloning that happens when an insect makes an exact copy of itself

phylum—a large group of living things whose bodies are organized in the same way

predator—an animal that kills and eats other animals

pupa—the larva during the stage in which it wraps itself in a cocoon or a case and stops eating and moving while its body undergoes a dramatic change in form (two or more pupa are called pupae)

scarab—a kind of beetle with a wide body that is often colorful, like Japanese beetles

species—a group of closely related living things that share almost every trait and whose members can mate and produce offspring that can also reproduce

Poetry Notes

Go Buggy!

This poem has four groups of lines; each group is called a stanza. Each stanza has a set of three lines that rhyme, and then a refrain. The refrain is the line repeated at the end of each stanza.

Hey There, Stink Bug!

This is a shape poem with all kinds of rhythm and rhyme inside and in between the lines of the stink bug!

Multiplication

The first two lines in each part of this poem rhyme with each other. They have four beats. Beats are the words or parts of words that give rhythm to a poem. They sound strongest, like the 'a' in aphid. The last lines of both parts of this poem rhyme with each other. They have five beats.

The Hot Shot

This one-stanza poem has lines that rhyme with the first line by using made-up words. Poets play with language!

Flies

Poets make up new forms of poetry to express their ideas. This poem has three stanzas that begin with four lines of almost all rhyme. Then each stanza finishes with a two-line rhyme called a couplet.

Japanese Beetle

Haiku poetry was first written in Japan more than three hundred years ago. In English, haiku usually have three lines of no more than seventeen syllables all together. Haiku poetry has a kigo, which means one or more words that help the reader figure out in what season the poem happens. In a haiku, the author can show how two different ideas relate in an interesting way.

Making Scents

Free verse is poetry that has no planned rhyme or rhythm other than the rhythm the poet hears as he or she develops and explores ideas and feelings. Poets use the space around words in their poetry to give rhythm and form to the way.a poem is experienced.

Nightmare

A ballad stanza has four lines. The first and third lines have four beats. The second and fourth lines rhyme and have three beats.

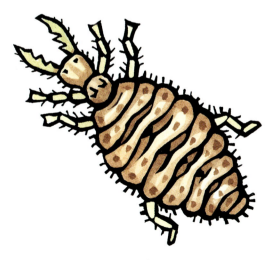

Antlion

This poem is a shape poem that uses the doodlebug's doodle, the shape of an antlion pit, and the path of the falling ant to make a poetry picture. The rhythm is three syllables in each beat, with the strongest syllable first, as in the word DOO/dle/bug. That kind of rhythm is called a dactyl.

Fooled by the Lights

This poem uses the colors of two kinds of firefly flashes to give more meaning to the words and ideas.

Advice to a Caterpillar

A limerick is a five-line poem that is meant to be funny. The first, second, and fifth lines have three beats each and all rhyme. The third and fourth lines rhyme together just like a couplet and have two beats in each line.

Swarm

A cinquain is a form of poem developed by an American poet who loved Japanese poem forms. It has five lines, with a specific pattern of syllables: two in the first line, then four in the next, then six, then eight, and finishing with two syllables in the last line.

Wolf Spider Mama

A Shakespearean sonnet has fourteen lines with five beats in each line. Each beat has two syllables: the first is quiet, and the second syllable sounds stronger. She LURKS/ in DARK/ly SE/cret CRACKS/ and CRAGS.

Dung Beetle

The tanka is a Japanese poem form even older than the haiku. It has five lines and no more than thirty-one syllables. Its ideas are usually from nature. Some of the words in a tanka can have more than one meaning in the poem. When you read a tanka, it can seem like two haiku poems—the middle line is part of each haiku.

Recycling

A clerihew is a funny four-line poem about someone, made of two rhyming couplets. In this poem the "someone" is the termite queen.

Thanklessness

A kyrielle has four-line stanzas that can rhyme in couplets or every other line. The second or fourth line is repeated in each stanza. Sometimes just the last word of the second or fourth line is repeated in each stanza.

Housekeeping

This poem has four rhyming couplets with seven two-syllable beats in each line.

Beetlemania

This poem is called a double dactyl. The first line of a double dactyl always has two nonsense words. The second line should include a proper noun—the name of someone or something. A proper noun is usually capitalized, but here it's not. One line in the second stanza of a double dactyl is all one word, like the word EN/to/mo/LO/gi/cal. Double dactyls are funny, and tricky!

Watch Your Step

The lines in this poem all end with a quiet syllable, like in the words MYStery and outLAST us.

Resources

On the Web:

http://www.fi.edu/qanda/spotlight2/spotlight2.html
The Franklin Institute's "Spotlight on Insects" includes links to detailed information on insect biology, ecology, identification, insect photography, and insect-human interactions. The site offers a "Hotlist" of entomology web links.

http://members.aol.com/YESedu/minimenu.html
The Young Entomologist Society (Y. E. S.) site, "Minibeast Museum," is a great place to learn about entomology.
The Y. E. S. publishes *CyberBugs Minibeast e-Magazine*, as well as the print magazine *Minibeast World*.

Books to Explore:

Insects. World Book Science and Nature Guides. World Book, Inc., Chicago, 2005.

A Field Guide to the Insects of America North of Mexico. Peterson Field Guides. Donald J. Borror and Richard E. White. Houghton Mifflin, Boston, 1970.

National Audubon Society Field Guide to North American Insects and Spiders. Lorus Milne and Margery Milne. Knopf, NY, 1995.

Acknowledgments

I would like to thank Dr. Cole Gilbert and Dr. Rick Hoebeke for their contagious enthusiasm and their review of my poetry and science notes.

The science behind these poems is based on a large body of entomological investigation that includes the work of Dr. Thomas Eisner and the work of Dr. Martha Weiss, who generously shared her seldom-seen photos of caterpillar frass.

So many thanks to those who encouraged this idea into a book: to the Hot Toddies; to my friends and family; to Steven Chudney; and to Charlesbridge for believing in gruesome insect poetry.